Echo

Edited by
Nick Houde, Katrin Klingan, and Johanna Schindler

T0243535

978 3959 054577

Content

Echo

Alphabets are tools for meaning making. Their value comes from systematizing abstract representations into analytic instruments—from witnessing and describing something to making things operational and manipulable. Linguistically, alphabets enable one to break down speech sounds into forms that are repeatable and recordable. More figuratively, alphabet-like structures break down phenomena into discrete and recombinant series that represent all of its component parts in a systematic yet open-ended manner. This way, alphabets can serve to recombine ideas or words into novel configurations that might enable one to act upon them.

But amidst the profusion of old and new processes of alphabet-making that characterize how the contemporary world is grasped, one quickly understands that such representations often overlook or occlude the values and purposes that underwrite them. After all, every attempt at alphabetization begins as an attempt to map and understand something for a specific reason. But what are those reasons and why use these representations and not others? And what values are imposed by using one alphabet over another?

The vast heterogeneity of representational systems that exist today—such as spoken or written languages, mathematical formulae, and graphic forms—implies political and ethical questions and decisions, as these representational heuristics are used to navigate and manipulate a catalytic planetary situation of mega-scaled technological infrastructure; of fragmenting geopolitics; of climate emergencies; and a crisis of care.

Starting from these problematic issues, this book compiles contributions that affirm values for the world-to-come by working through the fragments of the current one. This way, the essays and conversations not only challenge the nature of new alphabets but also articulate the role that value and purpose play in their construction and implementation. It seeks to tackle the many planetary-scale issues of our time to find common spaces for negotiation, for finding purpose, and for making forms of life that seem worth living on this planet between a multitude of perspectives and epistemologies.

The book experiments with the strange pairing of life and form. "If sound is birth and silence death, the echo trailing into infinity can only be the experience of life, the source of narrative and a pattern for history." Picking up on Louis Chude-Sokei's notion of the ECHO, the book attends to how the echo of past articulations of life and form has come to shape a world to come, both actively and passively; producing the technologies and ways of life that underpin the contemporary world. The book takes off from conversations had during the *Life Forms* event at HKW in 2019 by bringing some of their complexities into a new form.

The volume begins with the big bang as literary scholar Louis Chude-Sokei follows the sounds of creative forces, of technologies, and experience of life that have come to pattern history and the "human" narrative. His essay sets the tone and starts the sequence of texts and ideas that iteratively move through the echoes and consequences of planetary-scale technological development. This way, the texts unfold along the resonant trajectories and path dependencies that inform the values underpinning life and its relationship to form.

In their conversation, cultural scholars Luciana Parisi and Louis Chude-Sokei along with musicologist Gary Tomlinson address the role both the evolution of human cognition and planetary computation play in understanding differences between past and recent technological revolutions. This leads them to discuss how the historical trajectory of cybernetics and other forms of technological modes of thinking have produced a multiplicity of "we's," modulated by their pasts as much as the power dynamics that have shaped them.

Psychosocial theorist Lisa Baraitser works through the crisis of care confronting contemporary societies by reflecting on the management of the COVID-19 pandemic and the persistence of racialized violence that speaks to the psychosocial ramifications that riddle both our technologies and the political systems that operationalize them.

Experimenting with more-than-human and machine thought, media scholar Maya Indira Ganesh and artist Wesley Goatley discuss how bias automation has come to riddle many new technologies, carrying forth the troubling ideologies of the past and optimizing them within new technologies that increasingly guide many aspects of everyday life.

These different accounts lead into a coda in which historian of science Sophia Roosth and choreographer Xavier Le Roy engage in a conversation about life as a search term and how the connection surprise

reverse

between life and form influences their work both on a daily basis and in the context of the *Life Forms* event. The conversation was chaired by artist and researcher Sascha Pohflepp (1978–2019), who worked on, among other things, the recogonition and contingency of forms understood to be life.

Nick Houde, Katrin Klingan, Johanna Schindler

How Long Is an Echo?

To respond to the question, I will claim the privilege of quoting myself. However arrogant it might seem, I do so because these words published at the start of my career have followed and propelled me here and now function recursively as an echoing of what was first articulated in Jamaica as a willed echoing of cultural origins.

From *Dr. Satan's Echo Chamber* (1997):

Let me humbly begin with the history of the Universe. Western science has provided us with a myth of origins in the 'Big Bang' theory, which locates the beginning of all things in a primal explosion from which the stars, moons, planets, universes and even humanity are birthed. Because Western science's obsession with cause and effect has focused on the process of contraction and expansion in the universe (mirroring its colonial and neo/post-colonial conceits), it is the role of another kind of science to interrogate the metaphor in the term 'big bang.' Indeed, the fact that 'science' in the Jamaican vernacular is synonym for 'bush magic' or the occult, allows me to ground these metaphysics in the folklore of the Caribbean.

[...] the 'Big Bang' [...] is a sound, which makes possible the universe and then the world. Creation is merely an echo of that primal sound, a product of its sonic waves. This myth establishes one of the most crucial dialectics in human knowledge: sound and silence. What bridges the two elements is echo, the traces of creation. If sound is birth and silence death, the echo trailing into infinity can only be the experience of life, the source of narrative and a pattern for history.[1]

What has come to matter most is that this text told a story linking a black, "third world," popular music less to its commitment to rhythm, lyrical protest, or other conventions of hearing black sound, and more

---

[1]   Louis Chude-Sokei, *Dr. Satan's Echo Chamber: Reggae, Technology and the Diaspora Process*. Kingston: International Reggae Studies Centre, University of the West Indies, 1997.

to its direct engagement with machines and Western notions of technology. I have since termed this engagement a "black technopoetics," where technology is claimed and reimagined in ways productive to colonial peoples, thereby meriting a general reconsideration of media, machines, and the forms of knowledge based on them. In a "black technopoetics," for example, technology is also a conduit for indigenous, ancestral knowledge-systems, however fabricated and creolized, while also enabling a revised—also creole—Judeo-Christian (as in Rastafarian) eschatology. But more broadly, technology enables allegedly racial modes of knowing and is deployed in the Black Diaspora by a nationalism rooted in resistance to racism and colonialism, as well as in primarily male figurations of desire—for consumption, fulfillment, justification, or revenge. *Swag*.

The claim on rhythm and music as alternative and gendered racial epistemologies was certainly pioneered in American jazz earlier, in the twentieth century, as blacks found sound to be the only space where their political desires and historical imaginations were relatively unfettered; it was, after all, the only space available when formal politics were violently impossible. And though we may recall it as rooted in organic metaphors of improvisation, community, and performance, jazz was also a sign/sound of a modern, machine age. After all, black popular music in America emerges in the wake of sound recording, and it was arguably as crucial to shaping American Pop, first as a national then global form, as it was to rendering recording technologies themselves—such as the phonograph—as domestic, consumer products. Black sound helped machines and capital become far more intimate than thought possible before, collapsing the borders between self and other in the process of collapsing those between human and machine. In jazz, for example, blacks signified an urbanity and cool that whites would depend on for entrainment in their own modernity. This was a modernity (and modernism) that ironically marginalized blacks in order for them and their sounds to function as crucial signs/sounds of an increasingly inaccessible organic *outside* to a seemingly all-enveloping machine civilization.

Yet, in colonial Jamaica, these questions of time, technology, and race would go much further, via the construction of an indigenous mediascape on the margins of the racial landscape of both black and white America. Producers, musicians, writers, and thinkers in Jamaica would insist on centering these questions of time, technology,

race, and colonialism in listening. They would popularize these questions in shantytowns and ghettos before globalizing them, all the
while insisting that black practices of listening could perhaps be a
broader sphere of cultural and political possibility than a visual reg-
ister that had overdetermined blacks as animal and over-represented
"the human" as the indivisible property of whiteness.

Sound, then, was the key, the space of democratic potential,
as the great Ralph Ellison always insisted. And sometimes it was a
weapon. Music, however, was never the point. There was a primary
tool involved in this creation of a discourse, and it was and is the
master's tools that matter, and how those people never intended
for those tools to restructure them according to different priorities.
Because blacks were branded as tools during slavery, and because
they continue to be imagined and socially placed somewhere between
human, animal, and automaton (*machine*), the story of "black technopoetics" is ultimately about tools using tools. (As I have elsewhere
historicized, the very questions of whether robots or algorithms have
intelligence, personality, or just mimic/double humans, or if they
could possess souls and operate independently of their masters, were
the same questions asked of black slaves. These questions still haunt
and generate our narratives of technological development, from
science fiction and electronic music to robotics and AI.)

This story—my story—has always been about machines using
machines, upgrading their own consciousness, making themselves
human by forcing categories like technology and "the human" (not to
mention democracy) to expand beyond foundational expectations and
prejudices, and to do so initially via sound. In post-plantation Jamaica,
the tool in question was *echo*—rudimentary analogue tape machines at
first, all of which opened the way to digitization. Of course, echo as a
technique of "black technopoetics" prefigured Western technology: in
slave music, from the reverberations of drums that would be outlawed
for their subversive communicability, to the poetics of "double-speak,"
which black American critics call "signifyin(g)" and that W. E. B. Du
Bois would theorize as "double consciousness." Echoes, after all, are
dependent on *doubling*, one of the roots of *dub*.

Echo machines became available less than a generation after
political independence in Jamaica. These machines were glimmer-
ing signs of a technological revolution occurring elsewhere, but they
could connect the margins to the center's flow of information (back

when terms like "margin" and "center" made more sense than they do now; back when terms like "margin" and "center" were being revised, in fact, by the intimacy that echo and its machinations would create by collapsing space and time, them and us). These machines could also facilitate a more enduring political need in the black world: *metaphor*. Specifically, *racialized metaphors*, such as of space, of time, and of the ability to see the black colonial *self*, doubled and projected autonomously in a zone of your own creation.

From analogue tape to digital workstations, such projections operate against the dominant colonial structure of mimicry, wherein *the black* is merely approximate to the white/the human, its dark echo. The projections operated as a counter-mimicry, the reproduction of its own meanings (however fictional or romanticized). This featured a rejection of the privileged *chromatic* scale (and I intend for this pun to emphasize also the difference between color and sound, race and music). Echoic doubling—or racial feedback loops—constructed a space we can now legitimately call *virtual* but existed in sound as the primary nexus between race and technology, between a cultural origin obscured by chattel slavery and futures enabled by a deliberate reimagining of the master's machines.

So, it is through echo as a technique and appropriated technology of virtual self-reproduction that we trace the emergence of distinct black, non-standard, *creole* technologies—that "other kind of science" I alluded to earlier. This other kind of science may operate through sound and is rooted in race or racial encounters with machines, but it has become central to global culture and possible futures. After all, it was and always is in sound where blacks engage and inform cultural and technological revolutions, and so to reduce what they do to "music" is often a way of marginalizing technological innovation. It is a way of dismissing coding by hearing it as rhythm, ignoring programming by figuring it as instinctive play, and banishing black informatics to animal nature, instinct, or the organic. This is why to even answer the question, "How Long Is an Echo?" requires us to submit ourselves to the ears of the other.

Jamaican music was not the first or only music to fetishize echo or reverb. It is obsessively present in the blues, rockabilly, country music—all of which have left their traces on reggae, from its gun-toting masculinism to an obsession with wide open spaces in the productions of golden age *roots* (just check Bunny Wailer's *Blackheart*

Man or Bob Marley's *Natty Dread* for echoes of Nashville). But Jamaican music was the loudest and the most explicit about its ideological intent. Informed by anti-colonial and anti-racist politics (or rhetoric), the music enabled an amplification of racialized interiority via sound—belly-rumbling bass in particular—and through echo as sonic metaphor of cultural particularity and historical context.

Echo, after all, is rich in signification. From Ovid to Lee "Scratch" Perry, it is most obviously a sign of distance, of dispersal—all of which are appealing to a migrant and homeless people, who could only fetishize origins and arrival. Echo is also a sign of longing, loss, alienation, of haunting (the dead and the dying, the murdered and the guilty). In sound reproduction, echo is how space is reproduced. And for those who are denied land, movement, and access, space will always generate a delirium easily mistaken for freedom. But this is why it should come as no surprise that the music would so fetishize Africa, the Middle Passage across the Atlantic Ocean, the compressed silence of slave holds and dungeons, or, with hip-hop—the product of a Jamaican migrant techno-poetics—the metallic clang of prison bars, the sirens of law and carceral capitalism (the prison industrial complex, which in America is increasingly connected to large-scale migrant detention), and the dense urban spaces of corporate neglect. This is why I have insisted that pre-independence Jamaica ultimately prefigures our current moment via its focus on two of our primary and ongoing concerns: migration and technologization.

More intimately, echo signifies the space between self and other, us and them, origins and futures. It narrates between being and repetition (or replication), which is even trickier than nothingness, given the increasing realities of surveillance and the sudden knowledge that erasure, invisibility, and silence are increasingly difficult to achieve. However, as Leo Marx pointed out, echo is also a metaphor of reciprocity. Perhaps this is why the music provokes such physical intimacy. Because echoes emphasize space, amplified echoes can render even ghetto streets, tight enclosures, or basements so vast that bodies cling together rather than remain vulnerable.

But what does it mean to speak of reciprocity when we are speaking of echo, of racialized sound, of migrants policed by regimes, still unsure of their full humanity, of space increasingly privatized, retrenched, and vigorously surveilled? This is why we must remember from Ovid that the story of Echo is also the story of Narcissus, that

Echo was never free because "she" (as Gayatri Spivak reminds us in her notable attempt to "'give woman' to Echo") is always balanced by narcissistic forms of power.[2]

To speak of Echo, then, is to always speak of power and, of course, desire—which imply reciprocity but without the sheen of historical innocence or progressive utopia. Echo reminds us that we are all implicated in each other. For example, in Spivak the story of Echo and Narcissus is ultimately "a tale of the *aporia* between self-knowledge and knowledge for others."[3]

Aporia—that irresolvable contradiction, once too fashionable in our critical lexicon. For Caribbean thinker Édouard Glissant, it is not a contradiction but instead a necessary feature of how "thought makes music."[4] I will reverse Glissant's phrase here and say instead that "music makes thought," given that black intellectual and radical traditions have always depended on sound and therefore technology; and it is the creolization of the master's machines to make sound that enable his version of reciprocity, which he calls "Relation" in preference to solitary or solipsistic notions of "Being." For Glissant (as it is for me), *relation* is rooted in a migrant aesthetic generated by the Caribbean intellectual and radical tradition that fetishizes bodies in transit: "Relation is the knowledge in motion of beings," he writes, and it "strives toward the being of the universe, through consent or violence."[5]

More pertinent to our question, "How Long Is an Echo?" is that: "In Relation analytic thought is led to construct unities whose interdependent variances jointly piece together the interactive totality. These unities are not models but instead reveal the échos-monde."[6] Échos-monde is his term—world-echo—the complex and contrapuntal, noisy and silent relationships between and among cultures that construct the world:

2   Gayatri Spivak, "Echo," *New Literary History,* vol. 24, no. 1. (1993), pp. 17–43, here p. 17.
3   Ibid., p. 19.
4   Édouard Glissant, *The Poetics of Relation*. Ann Arbor, MI: University of Michigan Press, 1997, p. 93.
5   Ibid., p. 187.
6   Ibid., pp. 92–93. S. R.

In order to cope with or express confluences, every individual, every community, forms its own échos-monde, imagined from power or vainglory, from suffering or impatience. Each individual makes this sort of music and each community as well. As does the totality composed of individuals and communities.

Échos-monde thus allow us to sense and cite the cultures of peoples in the turbulent confluence whose globality organizes or *chaos-monde*.[7]

Scholars of sound might recognize sympathies here with Veit Erlmann, particularly his book *Reason and Resonance: A History of Modern Aurality*. They share a focus on sound's relationship to Western "analytic thought" as well as a dependence on sound as metaphor for philosophical and cognitive reciprocity, or as Glissant puts it, "interactive totality." But even in the face of genocide, he defines *world chaos* as a necessary *aporia,* a contradiction that—unlike for Spivak—merely feeds the larger, inevitable process of creolization that echoes represent. We are all implicated in each other, and we can never be free of each other.

Many readers often mistake Glissant's seeming acceptance of noise and chaos and echoes of echoes of echoes as an endless recursiveness that leads to passivity. They assume that, for him, reciprocity transcends the horrors of history and the predations of power that can be traced from European maritime exploration to the slave trade, from colonization to our crumbling global order. Admittedly, in his work, the complexities of cross-cultural interaction occur on such a vast scale that human activity seems easily dwarfed and inconsequential. However, the *échos-monde* is produced by racism and xenophobia just as it resists them. It features also the consolidation of exclusive "identities" due to static notions of culture, tradition, and limited conceptions of "the human," which all arise from those systems of power; but then also, it undoes them by its promiscuous blurring of borders, boundaries, bodies, and desires—something sound does in ways we have still yet to fully acknowledge or understand.

Were he here, Édouard Glissant, who precedes me in thinking about the poetics and politics of echo—which are the poetics of race

7   Ibid., pp. 93–94.

and sound—would likely say the length of an echo reaches from the violence of creation to its repercussions, those being the measurement and rhythm of history itself. On a more human, planetary scale, which has brought us here, that length is measured by the violence of human movement and its endlessly formative implications.

Where Do We Find
Ourselves?

A conversation on the conditio
humana and non-humana

Gary Tomlinson: Luciana, your work focuses, among other things, on understanding the logics and operations behind "planetary computation." I'd like to locate this computation in the *longue durée* of the human technosphere and its epochal shifts, highlighting the shift from technology as an extension of human somatic capacities to the technical formalization of reasoning in automated thought in the middle of the twentieth century. That shift seems to be summed up by the notion that tools came to be means of "concretizing logic." Now extend the perspective across evolutionary timescales, and epochal shifts appear that might show such concretizing even in the Paleolithic period. Let me exemplify this by contrasting two ancient technocomplexes.

One of them, the so-called Acheulean technocomplex, reaches back 1.75 million years. (Remember that our species goes back 300,000, at most.) To make an Acheulean handaxe you take a core stone and chip away at it with another stone, eventually fashioning a symmetrical biface with a cutting edge around it. Such tools have been dug up by the thousands—this was a hugely dispersed industry practiced by several or many species of hominins. But there's not a strong sense of system in producing an Acheulean biface; at each moment you size up the state of the core, deciding where to chip next. One could say that logic is concretized in this industry only in the weakest way.

Fast forward now to 350,000 years ago and the Levallois technocomplex, well studied in examples from Neanderthals and our direct African ancestors. This technology now requires you to choose your core carefully, and to then perform certain operations on it to prepare it for another hierarchical level of distinct operations, so as to ready it for a third level of operations. At this point, if you've done it all with expertise, you can, with one strike of the hammerstone, lop off a perfectly formed point, something to add on at the end of a stick to fashion an arrow or a spear. Here there seems to be at work a substantial concretization of logic, even a recursive and hierarchic logic. Of course, I'm not trying to deny huge differences between this and what occurs in information technologies in the middle of the twentieth century; but I wonder how it is that we can specify more clearly what that difference is? What's the new mode of concretizing logic that finally brings about planetary computation?

Luciana Parisi: There are two points that I can discuss in relation to your observations. On the one hand, I think this observation—that the concretization of logic was already present in ancient technocomplexes—can challenge the assumption that before modern epistemology there was a world without logic and that only with modernity did tools finally became mental activities rather than simply being an extension of physical action. Modern epistemology is indeed sustained by a universal model of technology which becomes the standard system of measurement against which the rest of the world must be subsumed. By claiming the exceptionalism of the concretization of logic in machines, industrial modernity imparted a universal model of technology as part of the epistemological justification for the operations of what Cedric Robinson calls racial capitalism, dependent on slavery, violence, imperialism, and genocide.[1] In other words, the question posed by Gary can enable us to critique and then counter-critique the modern universal model of technology. On the one hand, it cannot be divorced from the colonial and patriarchal epistemology that characterized the articulation of human reason in modernity and on the other, precisely through this standpoint, it can retroactively contribute to revisit the history of human technology against the universal history of racial capitalism.

From this standpoint, when Martin Heidegger reflects upon what is so modern about the concretization of logic in relation to the universal question of technology, he recognizes the configuration of a techno-concretization of causality that remains hidden from the linearity of cause and effect. Cybernetic system or the articulation of causality in terms of feedback.

---

1   See Lisa Lowe, *The Intimacies of Four Continents*. Durham, NC: Duke University Press, 2015, p. 149.

For Heidegger, the transparency of causality in the new cybernetic order of society shows an automated mode of decision-making that does not belong to the human although it does open the human up to a dimension of thinking beyond modern linear causality. I think of this automation of intelligence as a learning process where causality is distributed and dependent on its interaction with the outside; there are a lot of possibilities for reconstructing this concretization in terms of an incomplete logic without given Logos. The point is not to deny that logic was there to start with, but to accept that what became of logic in automated machines opened up logic to a capacity to transform the very condition of what logical thinking meant in modernity. So, how does the tool actually become an automated system able to learn and not just express some kind of given sequences of function, but also rather reactivate a function in response to the environment repeatedly? Within industrial capitalism, the difference between the steam engine and the automated assembly line becomes quite radical when considering the tendency of a cybernetic system that learns by feedback and of computational systems that meet the limits of computation in terms of infinities of propositions that cannot be programmed a priori. I'd say, then, that the difference with modernity is that causality becomes embedded and folded within the procedures of interactive feedback, which challenges precisely the condition of reason—the linear causality—of modern epistemology.

From this standpoint, while the concretization of logic in machines sustains the effective system of racial capitalism, it also exposes the incompleteness of universal formulas of mathematics. My point is that with modernity, such concretization brings forward the incompleteness of the onto-epistemological ground of the human, at least insofar as machines start to think beyond what they are programmed to do. In other words, the more the quest of knowledge or the scientific enterprise with its universal formula begins knowing the world, the more it enters the sphere of the unknown. The more it understands that the unknown cannot be contained within a given sequence of algorithms, the more the unknown becomes what has to be violently compressed and, at the same time, what continued to defy the illusion of a complete universal knowledge.

Louis Chude-Sokei: Ultimately, the question Gary is asking is what makes our technological revolutions and transformations different from those that happened before? History, indeed, if anything is a relentless series of technological transformations and transfers, even across borders unimaginable by the logics of Western computation, and certainly across borders established by its epistemes. Actually, this is what I think notions of "racial capitalism" tend to leave out, so focused are they on a too-rigid acceptance of a Marxian teleology or perhaps temporality. If in fact we can define technology as a multiple—and we most certainly should—there are then different types of technology, different types of technological thinking, perhaps different forms of techno-rationalism that go back into deep time, way back into the past. Such thinking informs modes of engagement and resistance at work, for example, among those who would become "conscripts of modernity," to use David Scott's fantastic formulation.[2] But what is it that makes our particular moment different beyond particular forms of hardware and specific sociopolitical arrangements of power that depend on that hardware to structure and delimit them? Luciana's concern is that there was a certain kind of break in the 1930s, '40s and '50s, with Cybernetics, and so the kinds of technologies and technological problems we have now are distinct from what we've had in the past. In my work, that "break" coincides with not only decolonization and specific anti-racist movements that are themselves critical of technology and its racial rationalism, but also the engagement with Western hardware by Blacks, particularly in and around sound production and music. I've referred to it as a politics of "echo," where for example, in Jamaica, the fetishizing of, say, "echo chambers" is explicitly done as an act of engagement with what we would now call virtuality, self-projection, and cultural amplification. Therefore, what makes the twentieth century and its

2   David Scott, *Conscripts of Modernity: The Tragedy of Colonial Enlightenment*. Durham, NC: Duke University Press, 2004.

technological revolutions slightly different from those in the past would have something to do with an increasing level of access to those revolutions from their own margins. For example, the birth of cybernetics—certainly I would date it to around 1950 with Norbert Wiener's *The Human Use of Human Beings*, and texts like that.[3] But the 1950s is also the period of massive worldwide decolonization. So again, there's a relationship between decolonization and the development of certain kinds of technologies, which happen concurrently and are engaged immediately from the margins, an echo if you will of colonial usages. If we don't connect these cross-cultural phenomena to each other, we have to acknowledge at the very least that that historical coincidence is indeed what makes this period different from previous technological revolutions and relevant to all imminent others.

Another example is that in the United States you also have major challenges to white supremacy, to patriarchy, we have all of these challenges to centrality, and technology is—as the wonderful Michael Adas always insists—crucial to the establishing and maintaining of white centrality (more so than "race" he'd argue). Also, in the context of European and Western philosophy and questions of knowledge and knowledge-making, we have the birth of things like post-structuralism and the critique of the subject, and the attempt to reimagine knowledge in nonhierarchical terms. The "Anthropocene" is another thing that makes this particular moment different, or perhaps the "Plantationocene," to remind us of its colonial and slave trade provenance. Plus, the people who are generating things like cybernetics, were themselves not immune to racism or unaware of race. Norbert Wiener spent a lot of time talking about slavery. He quite accurately understood that, if we are on the verge of creating new kinds of beings, new kinds of inhuman beings, or beings that will challenge our understanding of what is the human, the

3   Norbert Wiener, *The Human Use of Human Beings: Cybernetics and Society.* Boston, MA: Houghton Mifflin Harcourt, 1950.

only way we had to understand them are as beings seen
previously as inhuman, which are slaves. So African slaves
become central to how Wiener imagines cybernetics, and
how slavery—as a form of and anxiety about labor in capitalism—is transformed and extended. So if, in fact, there is
a difference between our moment and a previous technological moment, it is certainly due to shifts in power, shifts
in capitalism, shifts in how the West sees itself globally,
and technology becomes very much a part of that narrative.

GT: A notion that you discuss in your work, Louis, is "creole technologies." In relation to what we just discussed, I wonder how we
define or delimit some of those? I also wonder whether we could talk
of "creole technospheres," advancing the sense that the technosphere
could be subject to the same kind of multiplicity as technologies
themselves are. There's an extensive discourse in African American
scholarship and African scholarship about these technological multiplicities, isn't there?

LC: I would certainly love to, because in doing so we're
talking about multiple epistemologies, multiple modernities, which is a wonderful set of conversations, echoes of
each other as I like to say. I keep echoes and other such
metaphors alive simply because they implicate each other
and refuse any suggestion that these conversations and
epistemologies and modernities are ever discrete. I think
the turn to technological multiplicity is implied and present in much Black scholarship and thinking but is only
just emerging as a specific body of knowledge/mode of
critique. The dyad of race/technology, as I've termed
it, is still needing more attention, but the engagement of
the emerging category of "the human" via race and racial
formations (and gender, of course) is certainly front and
center now. But we also have to understand that there is
a dominant technosphere that impinges on all the others, a primary sounding, if you will, which might have
delayed the emergence of that thinking. That dominant
technosphere—in terms of activism and creating a global
consensus around environmental transformation as

being also connected to migration, gender, sexuality, and race—finds it difficult to incorporate multiple perspectives, simply because these are deeply distrustful of that dominant technosphere itself, which is the white European one. That is where technology continues to be defined, just as it has always been where rationalism and logic is defined. As we speak about creole technologies and multiple forms of knowledge around technology and multiple types of niche construction, we also have to talk about that elephant in the room.

So yes, this returns us to the "plantationocene," which Caribbean and Black scholars have been articulating for some time. The names that come to mind are C. L. R. James, Antonio Benítez-Rojo, and Sylvia Wynter, but it runs through a whole tradition in which to understand modern, Western subjectivity; so perhaps to imagine alternatives to knowledges based on it, it is necessary to understand plantation slavery as a global, world-making phenomenon. We tend to fetishize industrialization and the factory as that which constructs certain kinds of modern subjectivities and rationalities in relationship to technology. However, arguably the plantation was what created modern subjects and rationalized beings, because it was a machine, absolutely. What then is computational logic and niche construction from this perspective?

LP: Yes, and I guess the elephant in the room here is definitely to do with the lineage that one has to claim, refuse, or hack. What kinds of modernities are to be reinvented to bring forward an onto-epistemological alliance with servo-mechanical systems and claims for creole technologies? How would we break away from the universal history that subtends the monologic of the Anthropocene? These computational technologies emerge from a specific lineage. One can think about the slave ship—already a mode of formal computational logic insofar as the compression of randomness and the sequentiality of functions determined the system in terms of the linear enumeration of bodies, the data prediction of their exchange value, the parameters of costs versus killing and/or letting die—it's almost like a live database.

modulated

formless

My point, however, is that we can only think about this in terms of computational logic because we have a critical language today that allows us to think about it retroductively. That is, we can only deduce that the slave ship was a database because we know today that computation is not a tool but a logic of governance, discipline, and war, and because we know how industrial capital extended and accelerated racial capital by automating the model of the slave within the servo-mechanical systems of cybernetic feedback operations. Following Robinson,[4] one can argue that industrial capital has roots in the colonial empire with the industrialization of the plantation model of work, as Louis has just remarked. From this standpoint, what allowed the plantation model to become transubstantiated to Europe was precisely this kind of transfer of the metaphysics of enslavement, multiplied in the servo-mechanics of the assembly line, the zombification of the working class, the stealthy subjection of affective women's labor that sustained the work of the proletariat, and so on. There is a lineage, which can be mapped all the way forward to fantasy imaginings about the "coming age of the singularity,"[5] where the universal model of enslavement returns under the planetary call for full automation.

However, in my view, this lineage has to be counter-actuated by challenging the universality of technology and the epistemological pillars of recursivity, determination, sequentiality, and divisibility, which constitute the logic of computation. I am interested in further elaborating on creole computation when discussing what happened with computation and with cybernetics at this moment when the incomputable—or this kind of impossibility of compressing all that is unknown into a universal formula of analytics and history—also created what Denise Ferreira da Silva calls "the global idea of race."[6] What I mean by this is that the mathematical encounter with the incomputable also defined a counter-actuality of the colonial enterprise, which

4   Cedric J. Robinson, *Black Marxism: The Making of the Black Radical Tradition.* Chapel Hill, NC: University of North Carolina Press, 2005.

5   Ray Kurzweil, *The Singularity is Near: When Humans Transcend Biology.* London et al.: Penguin Group, 2006.

6   Denise Ferreira da Silva, *Toward a Global Idea of Race.* Minneapolis, MN: University of Minnesota Press, 2007.

epistemologically admitted the ingression of infinities, indeterminacies, and nonlocality into the matrix of capital. So, "Where do we find ourselves?" We find ourselves at this moment, this junction, where we have all these epistemological elements, all these mathematical-computational arguments for nonlinearity, indeterminacy, infinity, nonlocality, processual reasoning, and interactivity. These challenge the universal model of technology from within; rather, they expose the possibilities of redoing modernity, redoing the human, redoing the technosphere from the bottom and across multiplicities. Actually to argue that there was a servo-mechanical logic already dismantling the universal epistemology of modernity is also to argue that science and technology have been allies in the overturning of capital and its colonial and patriarchal recursive logic.

GT: We are it seems, increasingly aware of how our lives are controlled by planetary computation, by algorithms the likes of which we cannot begin to understand, and, also, struggling to recognize the legacy that Louis was talking about. We need now to elaborate a creolization of technologies and of technospheres across the world. Yet that creolization, the recognition of multiplicity, is exactly what fragments the resistance to the dominant technosphere that is so crucial. So, where do we find ourselves? How do we balance the need to recognize multiplicity with the need to assemble somehow, to form a coalition that can stand any chance against the multinational corporate coalition that sponsors planetary computation today?

LP: This question requires inquiry into the figuration of the human in its relationship with the inhuman. We know that the question of the human as a category is an imperative that has to be constantly rewritten so that everything can stay the same. But the horizon of the human is only there to be contested, overturned, and claimed back by collective technopolitical projects that refuse the monological racialization and genderization of the human. So, the project of the "we" cannot be a given, it needs a radical reconstruction outside the established category of the human. This category must be counter-actualized by the possibilities of a speculative "we," which stems from crossing logic, revising logic, dismantling logic to then unfold

the trans-temporality of multi-logics, multi-worlds, multi-uni-
verses. There must be many methods to achieve that. By which
I don't mean a plurality of discrete approaches brought together
in the name of the cause's totality. It means that through the con-
flicts and struggles, asymmetries and contrasts, causalities must
be changed. Abolishing systems "as we know them" entails the
account of how the inhuman enters the world and pushes the
image of another kind of human that fits no category insofar as
it is the result of socio-technical activities, which manifest the
incompleteness of (alien) metaphysics. With this in mind, we
cannot pretend some kind of coalition simply happens because
we belong to a universal human language or human history.

GT: I want to veer back toward the Anthropocene, which both of
you have already mentioned. The problem that Luciana cites of the
human as a category is, in a posthuman light, a question of the excep-
tionalisms of all species. Any species evolves through the feedback
mechanisms of niche construction: Organisms adapt to their niches
at the same time as they alter them, hence altering the selective
pressures that shape their adaptation. This mutuality is a constant
in the evolution of life on Earth. What determines the exceptionalism of a particular species, then, is a question of which aspects of its
niche are altered by its lifeways—which aspects come to be part of
the feedback loop between niche and organism. The exceptionalism
characteristic of *Homo sapiens* is that, through its dominant technosphere, it has created a single, global niche of which planetary computation is now a key part. The existential threat of *Homo sapiens*—to
itself as well as to so many other species—is that now this global niche
has incorporated meteorological and geological forces. What used to
impose controls *on* us is now controlled *by* us, but with devastating
consequences. The feed*forward* controls that determined the lives of
Paleolithic humans—climate change, for instance—have now become
elements in the feed*back* cycles of our making, spinning in ways that
we can't predict or direct. No other vertebrate species has come
close to such global niche construction, and this defines, for me, the
Anthropocene. This view of the modern global technosphere differs
from Heidegger's—Luciana mentioned him earlier—in an important
regard. Instead of indulging in cozy, romantic fantasies about the
(ancient Greek) human and its technical *aletheia*, and laments about

modern humanity severed from its own tools, divorced from to-hand-edness, I see all technospheres, even nonhuman ones, as instances of niche constructive feedback, and today's global human techno-sphere as differing from others in degree, not in kind. This helps put the human back in its place—one niche-constructive kind of organ-ism among countless others—even as it illuminates the devastating scope of human impacts.

> LC: Suddenly, I'm reminded of a wonderful question I was asked after a talk that I couldn't answer, but has haunted me ever since: "Why is it that we can't or don't care or respond with concern and energy to climate change?" The question came up after I'd been talking about attempts to protect the environment by applying legal "person-hood" to inanimate objects or natural phenomena—lakes and animals, for example. So, I wonder if the basic point and problem is this: Can we care for things we don't anthropomorphize? It is a question, ultimately, of how to establish what Luciana just called a "collective technopo-litical project." Is the question of our limited or lukewarm response to climate change less about logic or reason and more about how logic and reason make sense of bodies? Because we know that one of the ways to generate a lack of concern for the other is by defining the other as less than human. Is the reason we can't mobilize a global coalitional politics around climate change related to our difficulty in seeing the environment as a being? It should remind us of the enormous cultural and political effort it took in aboli-tionism to convince whites that, that global mass of writh-ing, faceless, black shapes were in fact discrete bodies, actual human beings. And it's an effort that continues!

LP: But this problem of how logic and reason can make sense of a body is fascinating, above all because it is a cognitive prob-lem, namely a problem that demands a revolutionary expansion of cognition and of the pillars of knowledge *tout court*. I agree that the material n-1 dimensions of bodies must challenge the ontological premises of the human and its particular epistemol-ogies (for instance, the Western formulations of cognition, both transcendental and computational) that sustain the universal model of technology as the ultimate concretization of the evolutionary exceptionalism of Man. Thus, the effort to rewrite, to rethink or expand scientific knowledge, one could argue, does not entail an ornamental updating of the modern version of the human category as we know it. Rather, it involves a collective technopolitical inquiry into the horizon of a general artificial cognition, which defies both the primacies of mathematical formalism or computational analytics and the neurobiological model of the brain. The point is not just about the how the anthropomorphization of things make them more human, but instead how to replace the universal pillars of cognition with trans-temporal and trans-cognitive coalitions between all the alien thought of the past and the future as much as of the alien humans and more-than-humans.

GT: Yes, this project seems to me crucial in understanding the commonalities among many, many species and thus expanding outward the connectedness of the human and nonhuman—and that effort jibes with a posthuman transversalism. But, typically today, and ever since the information revolution of the mid-twentieth century, the project is reverse-engineered, starting from the human and human computational systems and yielding the anthropomorphic emphases on exceptionalism, not commonality. The effort to envision engineering, not reverse-engineering, is what leads me to invoke evolutionary timescales.

> LC: I really appreciate your problematizing of crisis, Luciana, or the articulation of constant crisis as the mode of man, which, however, reiterates man as the center of it. However, it is very difficult not to see actual crisis when it comes to this question of where we are or how we have come to frame where we are in particular ways, which we hope will allow us to transform the pillars of cognition. (Always a tough act to sell and enact, in that ontological revolutionary gestures inevitably threaten us with a quietism born of a confrontation with that scale.) For me at least, "Where do we find ourselves?" is more humble: It's a crisis of the "we," who the "we" are. After all, whose pillars of

cognition? Those of us who have been refusing and reject-
ing these pillars since the birth of modernity? I'm grateful
to you for the possibility of this insight. How do we construct new "we's"? Can we construct new "we's" for the
sake of coalitional politics, given the abuse of identities
and "we's" that impinge on how we understand ourselves,
against other conceptions of who we are, and structures
of identity-formation that delimit access to the category of
human? Can we create a new "we," when in fact in order
for me to communicate with you, and you to communicate
with me, there are so many encoded histories that work
against each other despite our goodwill? It is a question of
cross-cultural and meta-historical trust, and this seems to
me to be part of the problem of fragmentation, which also
goes back to the 1950s and '60s moment. There's a way in
which post-structuralism is a critique of certain kinds of
reason, but once it gets picked up by scholars of color in
India, Africa, and the Caribbean it becomes very important in fragmenting the privileges of a white, central subject.
So, it becomes a part of what we now sometimes dismis-
sively call "identity politics," but it's important to point out
how that comes out of this very lineage we've been talking
about. Finally, to imagine or create a new "we" demands, I
think, a reckoning with that more recent history while also
engaging the much larger and more distant one that you
and Gary have both limned here.

Who Do We Care For?

The question of care—what constitutes care, who or what does or needs something called care, and why care fails—surfaced during 2020. Two situations unfolded synchronously, pushing care, which is so often marginalized, feminized, and racialized, onto the political agenda: the dramatically uneven and unequal distribution of care during the COVID-19 pandemic in which some lives were protected and others exposed to the virus; and the reminder of the ever-present lethal violence of racism, as news emerged of the brutal killings of George Floyd, Breonna Taylor, Ahmaud Arbery, and other Black Americans, leading to an uprising of protest about the mattering of Black life. As is now clear, forms of social abandonment that have long been known to affect vulnerability to ill-health—poverty, lack of access to healthcare and educational opportunities, racism, the traumas of forced migration—are asymmetrical, and therefore give rise to asymmetrical needs for care. When we are let down by social structures that are there to support us, the body suffers, but in its need for care it also makes a political demand. Bodies, in other words, are exposed differentially to overt harm or to death, but bodies also suffer ongoing inequalities that are unjust and demand redress.[1]

The question "Who do we care for?" is therefore always a question of social justice, and care and violence, whether enacted through modes of abandonment or outright brutality, are bound to one another in complex ways. The philosopher Adriana Cavarero tells us that vulnerability to harm is not the same as helplessness. The human body is permanently vulnerable to wounding, as long as that body lives, whereas helplessness is contingent, circumstantial. Yet this permanent opening to wounding is also a permanent opening to care: "Irremediably open to wounding and caring, the vulnerable one exists totally in the tension generated by this alternative."[2] Further, if we are wounded at the very point that care is needed then a certain kind of violence is enacted, a kind of horror. This is not just a social or political injustice, but also an ontological offence. When we open

---

1   See Judith Butler, *The Force of Non-Violence.* London and New York: Verso, 2020, p. 50.

2   Adriana Cavarero, *Horrorism: Naming Contemporary Violence,* trans. William McCuaig. New York: Columbia University Press, 2009, p. 30.

ourselves to another, or find ourselves open, or are compelled to make
ourselves open, we expose ourselves to care and harm at the same
point. Cavarero uses the infant as the paradigmatic figuration of this
vulnerability, but in a (post-)COVID-19 world there are many others:
keyworkers forced to work without protective equipment; imprisoned
populations who already face shortened life expectancies; children
who depend on school to provide the only meal of the day but find
school indefinitely closed; women trapped in situations of domestic violence under lockdown; those living in enduring conditions of
poverty who must make impossible choices between meeting basic
needs and exposure to the virus; and, as has become increasingly
clear in the global North, people of color—whether those working
life-long in the UK health service where they represent almost half
of all medical professionals, or those living in urban centers in the
USA who have a higher likelihood of not being able to access healthcare. Needing care whilst being vulnerable in these ways risks this
particular form of wounding, and to inflict harm where care is needed
is a violent act that destroys life's form.

What is care? Broadly speaking it is a set of psychosocial activities, a form of relational labor necessary not just for birthing and rais-
ing children, for sustaining and maintaining kinship groups and community connections, or enabling flourishing at the end of life, but for
maintaining all systems that work against destroying life's form. Care
is social reproduction in its widest sense, underpinning every aspect
of capitalism's proliferation. Although we can and should pay close
attention to the ways that states and economies "care" for citizens as
much as we must understand the ways they are violent towards them,
care nevertheless takes place at the level of the quotidian, the mundane
everyday. There is little glamorous about care. Often it *takes too much
time*, entailing the stilled, stuck, and suspended time of waiting, repeat-
ing, staying, returning, maintaining, enduring, and persisting.[3] Care
involves staying alongside others as time *fails* to unfold. When we overlook care that demands patience or is itself a practice that waits to see
what giving time to a situation may bring, then we fail to think carefully
about care. What we might say, then, is that care is bound up in particular ways with enduring time's suspension, and that it requires a form

---

3   See Lisa Baraitser, *Enduring Time*. London: Bloomsbury, 2017.

of knowing-about, or holding in mind the antithesis of care—failures to care, or the perverse pull to enact harm when care is most needed.[4]

"Care, caring, carer. Burdened words, contested words."[5] The line comes from Maria Puig de la Bellacasa's essay "The Disruptive Thought of Care." To address the question "Who do we care for?" we need to think through the question Puig raises about the relation between care and thinking, and the question of burden and contestation in relation to care. First, is care a practice of thought, an activity not only captured by its material and affective dimensions but by a form of "care-ful attention" that can bring on new ways of thinking? If so, what are the implications of mindful care, care with a history or memory, for instance; care, as Christina Sharpe puts it, which is both wakeful, conscious, aware, and yet chooses to stay in the wake of histories of trauma, particularly of racial trauma?[6] In what ways does care itself disrupt thought? Secondly, whom does care burden, and who and what contests care? How does one "contest," in a political sense, "carefully"? What do careful protest, careful revolt, and careful disruption look like? If care requires the capacity to go on, are care and rupture antithetical? And how do we understand social, political, or even psychic change through the endurance of the more monotonous and dull temporalities of persistence, preservation, staying, or holding, of waiting, and then waiting some more?

The global COVID-19 pandemic has highlighted what was already in plain sight: There is a structural problem with care in the current conditions of global capitalism, which maps onto a psychosocial tendency to deny dependency and the need for care. Dependency, Judith Butler reminds us, does not diminish with time. We are all born into a situation of radical dependency that we never outgrow, even as dependency is exacerbated for some

---

4   See Lisa Baraitser and Laura Salisbury, "'Containment, Delay, Mitigation':
     Waiting and Care in the Time of a Pandemic," *Wellcome Open Research*
     5-129 [online], https://wellcomeopenresearch.org/articles/5-129/v2,
     accessed September 22, 2020.

5   Maria Puig de la Bellacasa, *Matters of Care: Speculative Ethics in More Than
     Human Worlds*. London and Minneapolis, MN: University of Minnesota
     Press, p. 1.

6   Christina Sharpe, *In the Wake: On Blackness and Being*. Durham, NC:
     Duke University Press, 2016.

more than it is others.[7] Structurally, however, care is "in crisis" in the global North, and this crisis is an expression of the reliance of financialized capitalism on social reproduction that operates as its own internal limit.[8] Capitalism, Nancy Fraser argues, has its own "crisis tendency," which manifests currently as strains on care systems. On the one hand, social reproduction props up and sustains capital accumulation. It reproduces the next generation of consumers and workers and maintains the material conditions that allows capital to extract profit from living labor. On the other, capitalism's tendency towards unlimited accumulation constantly destabilizes the very process of social reproduction that guarantees its future. It fails to support or recognize care because it is not easy to make care more productive or efficient. It is time-consuming and shows up in capitalist terms as "useless," non-productive, and wasteful, running contra to the relentless drive towards profit and innovation. From this perspective, care, crisis, and capital are permanently entwined. Capitalism cannot do without care, any more than it can function outside the temporality of crisis. And as care must operate within the logic of capital, therefore, it is vulnerable to both permanent crisis, and capitalism without end.[9] If care is to disrupt thought (especially the denial of the fact that it is permanently needed), it would have to disrupt permanent crisis, and be able to offer an alternative temporality in which to think differently. It cannot simply mop up crisis. Burdened thoughts, contested thoughts indeed.

Permanent Crisis

The problem with positioning care as what mops up crisis is that care strategies which respond to crisis only lead to more crisis rather than a genuine alternative to the current situation. Janet Roitman unfolds

7   Butler, *The Force of Non-Violence*, p. 41.
8   Nancy Fraser, "Contradictions of Capital and Care," *New Left Review*, no. 100 (July/August 2016), pp. 99–117, https://newleftreview.org/issues /II100, accessed January 4, 2019.
9   Lisa Baraitser and William Brook, "Watchful Waiting: Crisis, Vulnerability, Care," in Victoria Browne et al. (eds), *Vulnerability and the Politics of Care: Transdisciplinary Dialogues* (proceedings of the British Academy). London and New York: Oxford University Press, forthcoming 2021.

this as a logic of crisis rather than a logic of care.[10] Our word crisis comes from an Ancient Greek word, *Krino*, which medics used to indicate a turning point in a disease where life and death were in the balance and a decision had to be made. It originally implied a form of judgement entailing a separation between one state and another. Yet, by the end of the eighteenth century, the term had shifted from a decisive judgement to a protracted social and political condition, the permanent oscillation between the crisis and strategies for "anti-crisis."[11] Historical awareness in European cultures—the awareness of a past that is not the time of the present or the future—emerges as a kind of "crisis" or judgement of time itself, a situation in which *Neuzeit* or the modern era is by definition separated from the past and orientates towards an open future. This is a process deeply intertwined with colonialism, empire, and the control of women.[12] "White time"[13] comes to dominate other temporal organizations of the world; cosmic time, geological time, soil time, indigenous time, women's time, queer time, to name a few. Care disrupts the thought of permanent crisis when it remembers or pays attention to the multi-plicity of temporalities displaced by white time.

Roitman reminds us that crises which feel at the time to be turning points of history (she uses the example of the 2008 financial crash, but we could add the COVID-19 pandemic and the ecological catastrophe set in motion during the early decades of the Anthropo-cene), determine what are established as historical events per se. His-torical consciousness means specifically that time is not understood

10   Janet Roitman, *Anti-Crisis*. Durham, NC: Duke University Press, 2014.

11   Roitman draws on Reinhart Koselleck's conceptual history of crisis. See Reinhart Koselleck, "Crisis," *Journal of the History of Ideas*, vol. 67, no. 2 (2006), pp. 357–400.

12   See Dipesh Chakrabarty, "The Climate of History: Four Theses," *Critical Inquiry*, vol. 35, no. 2 (2009), pp. 197–222; Giordano Nanni, *The Colonisation of Time: Ritual, Routine and Resistance in the British Empire*. Manchester and New York: Manchester University Press, 2012; and Silvia Federici, *Caliban and the Witch: Women, the Body and Primitive Accumulation*. New York: Autonomedia, 2004.

13   Charles W. Mills, "White Time: The Chronic Injustice of Ideal Theory," *Du Bois Review: Social Science Research on Race*, vol. 11, no. 1 (2014), pp. 27–42; and Charles W. Mills, "The Chronopolitics of Racial Time," *Time & Society*, vol. 29, no. 2 (2020), pp. 297–317.

just as a medium in which histories take place, but that history is a temporality upon which one can make a judgement—one can "diagnose" what has gone wrong in the past and therefore act upon it.[14] The more historically conscious "we" become, the more we feel in crisis, Roitman tells us, and this provides the moral imperative to act now in the name of the future, to put right what has gone wrong. However, in *Neuzeit* the terrible paradox is that we can only lurch from crisis to crisis as the very condition of the contemporary. To be in the "now" is to live in the suspended time of prognosis. Crisis narratives themselves cannot produce alternative narratives or histories, as by definition, they are forms of judgement or critique. How, then, can we think of a future without crisis? Roitman asks, "How can we imagine that which fundamentally *excludes* our judgement, that *which calls for no decision*?"[15]

Perhaps our capacity to imagine that *which calls for no decision* can be understood as a practice of care? Perhaps care is a form of mindfulness or concern that precisely suspends the time of decision, the insertion of inaction within the time of crisis. Understood in this way, care would open up a different kind of time from *Neuzeit*, a form of "waiting time." Indeed, Achille Mbembe has written about the universal right to breathe during the COVID-19 pandemic and how the hiatus produced by the pandemic necessitates another kind of hiatus, one that suspends white privilege and the ongoing inequalities of the world:

> At this juncture, this sudden arrest arrives, an interruption not of history but of something that still eludes our grasp. Since it was imposed upon us, this cessation derives not from our will. In many respects, it is simultaneously unforeseen and unpredictable. Yet what we need is a *voluntary cessation, a conscious and fully consensual interruption.* Without which there will be no tomorrow. Without which nothing will exist but an endless series of unforeseen events.[16]

14   Janet Roitman, "The Stakes of Crisis," in Poul F. Kjaer and Niklas Olsen (eds), *Critical Theories of Crisis in Europe: From Weimar to the Euro.* London and New York: Rowman & Littlefield, 2016, pp. 17–34, here p. 19.
15   Ibid.
16   Achille Mbembe, "The Universal Right to Breathe" trans. Carolyn Shread, in *Critical Inquiry*, "In the Moment," blog (April 13, 2020), https://critinq.wordpress.com/2020/04/13/the-universal-right-to-breathe/, accessed July 18, 2020.

A series of unforeseen events is not a future. Although Mbembe's call may appear to be to "do nothing," a collective consensual cessation may allow "crisis" to operate as a non-place in the formulation of the question (What has gone wrong?) in order to open up the possibility for a future, for "something else," to emerge.

Depressing Time

What are the conditions in which we may be able to bear a collective interruption necessary to establish the universal right to breathe? The Invisible Committee suggests that in conditions of "crisis capitalism" the majority of the world's population are kept in a "chronic state of near-collapse" making it difficult to either stop or go on, but instead instilling a kind of staggering-on in a depleted exhausted manner.[17] In these conditions one could at least imagine a collective diagnosis of crisis, which might then give rise to some form of collective action, a coming together of all those who suffer from the current crisis in the technosphere, although to do so would require contending with exhaustion and depletion. To "stop" surely means collectively to bear these feelings, understood as atmospheres, or "structures of feeling"[18] that organize a historical era. Affective regimes can of course be countered by mobilizing opposing affects; exhaustion could be tempered, for instance, by hope. A. T. Kingsmith describes the potential of "reactive affects" to produce collective action.[19] Whilst capitalism pushes populations to take on anxiety and fear, to accept individual responsibility for collective crises such as rampant inequality and climate emergency, so activism could mobilize anxiety more collectively, interrupting its dominant construction and its debilitating effects on individual lives. Then outrage could replace fear and anticipation, or hope could replace sadness.[20] Yet, I worry that even affective anti-crisis will only lead to more crisis, rather than

17   See The Invisible Committee, *Now.* New York: Semiotext(e), 2017.
18   Raymond Williams, *Marxism and Literature.* Oxford: Oxford University Press, 1977.
19   A. T. Kingsmith, "We the Affectariat: Activism and Boredom in Anxious Capitalism," *Rhizomes: Cultural Studies in Emerging Knowledge*, no. 34 (2018), http://www.rhizomes.net/issue34/kingsmith/index.html, accessed January 4, 2019.
20   Ibid.

the elusive emergence of "something else." I would suggest instead that "something else" emerges in a rather counterintuitive way if we begin to think through the potentials of engaging with depression and de-pressing time.[21] Collectivizing depression would not entail replacing it with hope but sharing the exhaustion and depletion. De-pressing time would be less about slowing the frenetic rush of capitalist time and more about taking care of what COVID-19 has taught us: that the interruption of unequal life forms requires time's suspension, the collective, fully consensual interruption of how things have been whilst sidestepping the impulse to "fix" the crisis.

The English psychoanalyst Donald Winnicott makes a distinction between the *depressive position*; *depressive mood*; and *depression as illness*.[22] The depressive position is a psychoanalytic term for a state of mind in which we come to accept some responsibility for wanting to attack and harm the very same thing we love and depend on. It describes the capacity for ambivalence and mourning. A depressed mood can only be experienced if the ego has some rudimentary structure, some psychosomatic unity or what Winnicott calls "unit status." "Something" has to feel depressed. If this "something" is intact then depression can come to have meaning and value, so much so that within the experience of depressed mood one can access the seeds of recovery. Depressive illness, on the other hand, represents a breakdown of the processes that might enable the achievement of depressed mood. The clinical condition termed "depression" is associated with sensations of depersonalization, hopelessness, exhaustion, depletion, and futility. These affects belong to the psychic time that lies outside the capacity for concern, a time before the things to come matter to us. And the capacity for concern relates to the fate of our own destructive, violent, and aggressive impulses towards that which we love and depend on—it is premised on whether the loved object does or doesn't survive our psychic attacks. Paradoxically, a patient in psychoanalytic

---

21   For an extension of this argument see Laura Salisbury and Lisa Baraitser, "Depressing Time: Waiting, Melancholia, and the Psychoanalytic Practice of Care," in Elisabeth Kirtsoglou and Bob Simpson (eds), *The Time of Anthropology: Studies of Contemporary Chronopolitics*. London: Routledge, forthcoming 2021.

22   Donald W. Winnicott, "The Value of Depression," in *Home Is Where We Start From: Essays by a Psychoanalyst*. New York: W. W. Norton & Company, 1986, pp. 71–79.

treatment can only recover from a depressive illness if the analyst gets to know something about their *own* depression—we could say a *collectivized* depression. Knowing something about depression means that depression has held some meaning and has value through experiences of the survival of the analysts' own objects, internalized as rudimentary structure or form for what we could call "drive," or "life." Therefore, "life form" in this psychoanalytic sense is the capacity for depressed mood, as distinct from depressive illness. De-pressing time describes a capacity to go on knowing about crisis but without moving into anti-crisis, without attempting manic repair. Instead, the task might be to foster forms of connection that hold together care and violence so that they can know about one another; waiting with, enduring with, staying with, staying alongside, through the continual capacity to suspend judgement. This is less the time of indecision and more the time of *suspended* decision.

The turn to the clinic rather than the social or political scene is always a little uncomfortable. Time on a psychoanalytic couch day after day is perhaps a preeminent example of a "waste" of time in capitalist terms, a class-bound anachronistic practice well past its sell-by date. But I would suggest that the long, ongoing, relentless, working through of the double yet disjunct time of the analyst's and patient's depression may be oddly suggestive for attempts to think about how to stay in the hiatus that Mbembe is suggesting. In knowing about their own depression, the analyst's position is not to convince anyone of anything. This lifting of judgement and decision allows a form of repetition that may look like dead or depressed time—repeatedly going over the same old things—but is a way of "working through" time. It is not exactly anti-hope, but it is about being in a space that is outside of crisis and anti-crisis, the time perhaps of "something else."

This essay was developed in collaboration with colleagues working on the research project "Waiting Times," supported by the Wellcome Trust [205400/A/16/Z] (see waitingtimes.exeter.ac.uk). I am grateful to Katrin Klingan, Johanna Schindler, and Nicholas Houde for their kind invitation to speak at the *Life Forms* conference at HKW, Berlin, in 2019, and for their support with developing the ideas in this essay.

"It isn't about removing bias but keeping bias in."

This conversation took place on June 28, 2020, via a call on the Signal messenger app. The audio recording of this conversation was transcribed by Google's widely used machine learning speech-to-text engine; we edited the text for clarity. We also selected excerpts from the original, unedited speech-to-text transcription and included them in this edited version; they are underlined.

—Wesley and Maya

Wesley: So, it's nice to be able to come back to what we were talking about at the *Life Forms* conference in 2019,[1] with a lot of humans in the same room, sitting very close to us, which feels like a very strange version of the world here in June of 2020. In the spirit of this theme of the "echo," could you give a brief overview of what we spoke about then?

Maya: Yes I'd be happy to. What we spoke about last time was the "human," which digital technologies like AI are thought to simulate. I think what we wanted to focus on was about the state in place of the human and Lord of our conversations related to the place of the actual human. And that made us question which kinds of humans we have referred to under the category of "human." Because not all humans are the same, it turns out.

WG: Yeah, and I remember we were critical of metaphors for AI, and machine learning more broadly, which impart very human traits and tendencies to these systems. For example, we were talking about how when people describe these systems as being "agents," it gets into some tricky territory that might imply they have an agency and power which is nonhuman, or more-than-human. The people who really benefit from that narrative are the people who make and deploy these systems at the highest levels, which is inevitably governments and extremely powerful and influential corporate bodies. Our takeaway was that, in this way, language plays a key role in cloaking the power and abuses of these technologies in the powerful metaphor of having

[1]   See Life Forms, April 25–27, 2019, https://www.hkw.de/en/programm /projekte/2019/lebensformen/lebensformen_start.php, accessed October 31, 2019.

burn

figure

more-than-human or even superhuman capacities, framing them as being beyond our understanding or critique.

> MG: Maybe the thing you would just saying about agency in the discussion about agency and that's red. When we're saying "agency," what the governments, corporations, or the powers that be which make these technologies want is for us to think of agency and AI as qualities inherent to a technology not things that are made by February intentionally; Lucy Suchman says this.
>
> So it's like agency is not a thing that something *has*, it is what something *does*. So yes, nonhuman things—like this audio recorder, this microphone, like artificially generated, simulated voices—these have agency in that they can influence or shape things.
>
> We are connected to other things and other people through which we do things, so I want to return to that conversation about agency again and think about this tension with respect to how we want to think of ourselves as autonomous agents to do things independently, but actually we are very densely connected to each other. And this is where one of those problematic narratives comes up; you know there are some humans who have more power than others and perhaps imagine that they are sort of independent or autonomous agents. And they imagine technology for people like themselves and their little worlds. There's a well-known piece called a eyes white guy problem in which the scholar kid Crawford sourav identifies problems with bro culture and figures of boy kings like Mark Zuckerberg or Elon Musk who are examples of this.
>
> And actually the resistance to these people and their tech doesn't come from creating more figures like them, but from and by people who are very densely networked, who are not independent agents, but are interacting agents. I'm thinking about Worker movements and resistance coalitions and protesters.

WG: I totally agree with what you're saying about how agency is a form of action. I suppose that when I'm talking about this use of "agency" and "agent," I'm specifically thinking about conversations that seem to center on "the machine" as a beyond-human entity: what does it know, what does it see, can it think, can it make art, etc. In this, it's like there's a sort of Immaculate Conception at play, as there's always so little mention of all the humans who have gone into making a thing function exactly the way that it does.

I saw a tweet recently, something like: "I don't know why they called it 'machine learning' when it should be called 'bias automation,'" and that particular framing is such a clear way to describe and understand these technologies. In contrast to a phrase like "smart AI," "bias automation" refers to the recursive, recurrent loop of bias present in these technologies, which at least makes it a term that helps us to think about what these things actually are, instead of what their mythologies are.

That's why I took issue with that word "agency"; it dissolves the human behind the system, including the load of white guys that Kate Crawford illustrates. That sort of language doesn't help to bring those people to light. I still think that's one of the most interesting things about many public-facing discussions around AI, in that they feel somewhat bogged down in the notion of bias. The topic obviously now feels very known to those of us who've been working in this field for a while, but <u>do you know he still needs more unraveling I think of the recurring automation the color black boat Oreck nature of automation</u> when you have US politicians like Alexandria Ocasio-Cortez talking about bias in algorithms; but there is still more work to be done there.

I think of the metaphor of recurrence and of the "echo" as such an interesting way of thinking about this process of the same dumb ideas and dumb prejudices being recycled over and over again through the same shitty datasets; though I'm wary of throwing more stones of meta falls into this particular Paul. But I do think there is some value to metaphor; perhaps that's why I'm still an artist, and haven't just descended into a cave to become a hermit, because I still think there is real power and value in metaphor as an emancipatory tool.

MG: I agree with that, but something else I want to pick up on is how metaphor is so critically important in the formation of new fields of study. It's well established in the academic literature that when we're faced with new and uncertain scientific and technological discoveries and inventions, we rely on metaphor to make sense of things because they're taking place at scales and in ways that we don't understand.

So you know the weather with talking about Sir of the Earth's crust is a thin caramel like you don't like hardened layer of caramel underneath you know that's on top of this viscous liquid and you thinking about crème brûlée! So we are constantly in the realm of metaphor. And I think there's something beautiful about how scientists use these metaphors. I read about when they started protein folding in biotechnology, they would say things like "imagine this chain of proteins is like a card and you fold it;" and it's like, they're dealing with scales and things that are definitely not like cards and napkins! Robert Boyd writes about how when scientists talk about proteins folding, the metaphor allows them to think about what happens with the two edges of the napkin that come together. This idea, that two edges of the card come together when you fold them, allowed for breakthroughs in the science of protein folding. So metaphors are not only allowing us to understand, but also to push forward research in science. And sometimes I wish that in the fields of applied science there was more connection between metaphor and the actual making of things.

So, to go back to what you were saying, I love that thing about bias automation. There's bias being automated in, so there's also bias being automated out. How we think about actual social bias, then, is that we think we can compute it out. But in a way that has not thought through what bias actually means. What it means to have and to accept bias. This is where the realm of metaphors becomes very shaky for this field. Because, actually, there's a lot we understand about social bias already because there's been a lot of study of human society already. So let me give you an example of soda you know by a sorta mation in means bias automation out.

I got a new iPhone a couple of months ago as a birthday present, just around the time of the first pandemic lockdown. I was very excited because it is my first iPhone. I was setting it up and then came across Siri, the digital voice assistant. Now I have Siri on my Mac yet haven't enabled it, but there it was on my phone. I thought, well, let's check this out for once. So my partner has an iPhone, and he has Siri enabled for things like: Hey Siri, what's your best recipe for sambar? The first time I heard him ask Siri something, Siri responded with an Indian-accented

English-language-speaking man's voice. My partner said: Thank you Rahul, after he got the recipe. (Rahul is a common Indian Hindu name.) I started laughing and said: Your voice assistant sounded like an Indian man. He said: Yes, this is Rahul, my digital assistant! So when I was checking out my own new Siri to see what the options were, I discovered that I could choose a woman's Indian-accented English-language-speaking voice. I got excited even though I knew I would only use it for things like finding recipes. So the other day I said: Hey Siri how do you make shrikhand? Shrikhand is a dessert that's made from hanging yoghurt overnight, and then mixing in powdered sugar and mangoes; it's really delicious. And Siri replied: Hmm, here's what I found for "sure reckoned." Now, "sure reckoned" doesn't sound like shrikhand; but shrikhand sounded to the voice assistant like "sure reckoned." For a few seconds I was confused, because somehow I believed that because Siri's voice sounded like an Indian woman, then it would understand my Indian woman Voice sign saying show me a recipe for sweet corn. But just because it sounds like an Indian woman doesn't mean that the database that the voice assistant is drawing from is actually populated by things like shrikhand which are familiar to Indians; or how Indian women pronounce things. So it was a revelation to me. And because of the work that I do and things I understand about these systems, I was just sort of surprised at myself. Why did I think that because Siri has an Indian woman's accent option, that it is actually responding to me? Because it's not responding to me at all, the database doesn't know which weekend is. So that was my example of bias being automated out. And I want to end with this provocation that comes from the work of a computer scientist-friend, Zeerak Waseem, which isn't about removing bias but keeping bias in. That this is how I talk, this is my accent, this is what I sound like—and keeping the bias of that in is important.

WG: Absolutely. I also get frustrated with this notion that comes up in certain conversations that "we need to get rid of the bias in AI!" Because it's impossible: it's which bias, and whose biases are making these technologies what they are, these are the questions.

Life as a Search Term

Coda

In preparation for the *Life Forms* event in spring of 2019, the team at HKW brought together historian of science Sophia Roosth with choreographer Xavier Le Roy for a conversation about how they have come to understand the connection between life and form, elucidating how and why they structured their own contributions to the *Life Forms* event in the way they did. HKW asked participating artist and researcher Sascha Pohflepp to lead this conversation considering his own profound investment in issues related to life and form, on Earth and beyond. After his passing the summer after the event, to which he had contributed one of several major pieces he developed for and with HKW, his fascinating work on forms of life and technology lives on through The Post Rational Foundation.

Below is an excerpt of this interview, meant as a prefigured echo of an event, and a conceptual landscape, which was ephemeral and hard to capture due to its emergent structure and conversational tone. The accompanying diagram loosely depicts the spatial form of the event by considering how performers, the general public, and the contributors would converge within the auditorium over the course of the day.

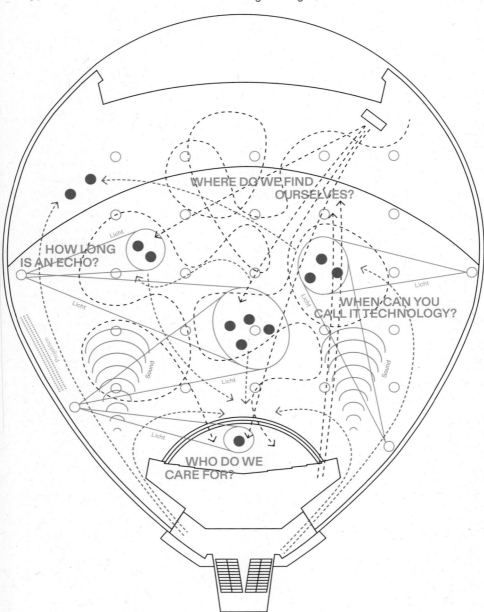

Sascha Pohflepp: The concept of life has been shifting throughout history. Are we then perhaps not actually looking for life but instead searching for something else, for which "life" might be the placeholder —like a search term?

Sophia Roosth: One of the things I'm continually struck by is how much the question of "What is life?" has changed, even in the last 200 years. From the idea of life as the series of functions that are resistant to death, to life as a negative entropy: life has always been defined by its limits and by its antonyms, such as the inanimate or inorganic. In the current moment, I think so much of what has counted as life is delaminating from context. This is partly because of genomics and the ways in which computing and big data have been enrolled into the life sciences. When life becomes this slippery category, people fashion new forms and definitions of life by reference to things that may or may not count as life. In relation to this, form can become a proxy for all sorts of other things, like complexity or pattern. Form and life have run against one another, and their definitions have merged and then pulled apart at particular moments throughout the history of biology and the life sciences.

Xavier Le Roy: I like this idea of life as a search term. My understanding of life is something that always involves a process of transformation.

SP: Sophia, since you are an anthropologist of science now teaching as a historian of science, and Xavier, you are a molecular biologist by training now employed as a choreographer, how did you end up working on life forms? Where did the idea come from, and how will you each work with it in your contributions for the event at HKW?

SR: My contribution is framed around the paper "Life Forms: A Keyword Entry," which I wrote with Stefan Helmreich. For this article, Stefan and I were examining how exactly definitions of life are particular to specific communities of practice. We were trying to understand the history of how the term "life forms" was used and how it differs from forms of life, which is a traditional social-scientific idea. How has our understanding of the term changed over time? For the event, I'm going to be leading a series of dialogues and conversations with allied thinkers in the humanities, social sciences, and the arts, trying to explode these terms of life and form while also trying to think about how people across disciplines have made different use of them.

> XLR: We will use the work *Temporary Title,* 2015 as the basis for our contribution. It will serve as a way to introduce and link certain interventions within the event. The work is conceived as an exhibition where visitors enter and leave at will. It tends to deal with the experiences of cycles and perpetual transformation, which aren't perceivable as such. There isn't a direction to follow, it's a situation where things emerge and disappear, moments where "things" happen to us. One attempt is to see how this work could draw together the questions discussed in the conversations conducted by Sophia.

SP: How are you tracing the transformative processes you've mentioned in your work?

> XLR: We want to draw attention to the transformations that we don't see or hear. The modes of moving organize each body and its actions, they are associated with operations that are both deduced from these movement principles and induced by other rules, which put in motion how each one of us relates and moves in relation to other individuals, the group, the space, and the duration of the event. We compose forms out of the rules that are used to move. We look for the specificity of something that is alive, which, therefore, is transforming with different agencies.
> The notion of landscape is a means to compose the actions and situations we create. We invite visitors to be in the landscape and experience it as the correlation between the still and the mobile, between what has form and what is formless, what is recognizable as a human figure and what isn't, between distance and proximity, naked and clothed.

SP: What role does scale play in looking at the way humans work alongside agents that are often invisible, such as microorganisms, Sophia?

SR: I think scale is another way of describing what kinds of forces are acting and at what level. One of the common denominators for my research is that I don't limit myself to paying attention to human agency in the anthropocentric sense of how anthropology was carried out historically. Rather, I tend to pay attention to nonhuman actors that are alive, like microbes or potentially viruses, but also inorganic substances, larger assemblages, or structures.

SP: Sophia, you wrote in the article you mentioned earlier about life as an aesthetic possibility that comes out of different processes. How do humans in practices like synthetic biology imagine the "future-types" that are described in your article? How do these explicitly future-oriented practices imagine what life could be?

SR: I think a lot of constructive biology—synthetic biology in my case—is trying out future definitions of what life may be by making new forms of life in the present. What is the definition of life, or what is the kind of life that we ourselves have already made? The research I'm currently undertaking with geobiologists—researchers in the Earth and life sciences—into what life is, is thought about by reference to the deep past. It's about scaling large traverses of time. How do you think about the aesthetics of life across three billion years in either direction? How would we begin to recognize what life looks like at that scale when thinking about an Earth or a landscape, in so far as life is adapting to the space that it occupies? How would we even know what to look for?

SP: Could simulative techniques, like artificial intelligence or genetic algorithms, significantly influence the search for form within life because they operationalize a sort of nonhuman imagination? Could they even help us to imagine forms and potentially feed them back into the envelope of life's possibilities?

SR: All of these things—whether using AI or a genetic algorithm —are human constructions. They're going to operate within the bounds of human construction, human designs, and human flaws, because the kinds of questions we ask are always curtailed or limited by how the program itself has been designed. I find it unlikely that such things will produce something that really has the capacity to surprise us. That reminds me of what the historian of science Hans-Jörg Rheinberger said about experiments: They're machines for making the future, and they're generators of surprise. In some way, therefore, those two things are bound together.

SP: Xavier, could your performances also be machines in that sense, or would you completely disagree with that?

XLR: I agree with that. A human creation, like a "machine" or artificial intelligence, is limited by the very fact that it was thought up by humans. The situation we create with a performance has similarity with that. It can be observed as a living form that is designed by the rules and tasks that organize it. In our choreography, we perform in a way that doesn't reduce our performance to an execution of the tasks. We try to build a situation where forms or events can emerge or happen to us, to the public as well. In these moments, the rules perform us as much as we perform them. Maybe that's similar to a machine that is producing surprises which are not necessarily the by-product of our will; it wants to challenge or question our understanding of what humans can do but within the limits of the humans that set it up. It might, nevertheless, produce unexpected forms and relationships between us as well as between the public and the performers.

+   Katrin Klingan is a literary scholar, curator, and producer of
art and cultural projects. Since 2011, she has been a curator
at the Haus der Kulturen der Welt (HKW), where she heads the
Department of Literature and Humanities. In this capacity, she
has developed and realized parts of *The Anthropocene Project*
(2013–14) as well as the long-term research project Anthropocene Curriculum (since 2013) which explores, in an experimen-
tal manner, new forms of knowledge. Her recent projects at
HKW include Mississippi. *An Anthropocene River* (2018–19), *Life
Forms* (2019), and The Shape of a Practice (2020).

+   Nick Houde is a researcher for the long-term projects
Anthropocene Curriculum (2013–present) and *Technosphere*
(2015–19) at the Haus der Kulturen der Welt. Outside of HKW
he has taught at various schools in Europe, including Bard
College Berlin, Zurich University of the Arts, and the University
of Applied Arts in Vienna, and is lead investigator for the
Vertical Union Working Group at the research- and network-
platform Trust. Formerly, he has written articles, given public
lectures, and performed music under various monikers.

+   Johanna Schindler is a postdoctoral researcher at the
WÜRTH Chair of Cultural Production at Zeppelin University, Fried-
richshafen, the managing editor of the *Journal of Cultural
Management and Cultural Policy*, adjunct lecturer at the University of Connecticut and freelance translator and editor.
Previously, she has worked as a researcher and coordinator of
the project *Technosphere* (2015–19) at the Haus der Kulturen
der Welt, Berlin.

+   **Lisa Baraitser is Professor of Psychosocial Theory in the Department of Psychosocial Studies, Birkbeck, University of London, and a Psychoanalyst, member of the British Psycho-analytical Society. She is the author of the award-winning monograph *Maternal Encounters: The Ethics of Interruption* (2009) and *Enduring Time* (2017) and has written widely on motherhood, care, and time. She is currently Co-Principal Investigator of "Waiting Times," a five-year cycle of research on time in healthcare, funded by the Wellcome Trust.**

+   **Louis Chude-Sokei teaches at Boston University where he directs the African American Studies Program. He is also the Editor-in-Chief of the leading journal *The Black Scholar*, and founder of the sonic art and archival project *Echolocution*. His work includes the award-winning *The Last Darky: Bert Williams, Black on Black Minstrelsy and the African Diaspora* (2005), *The Sound of Culture: Diaspora and Black Techno-poetics* (2015), and the forthcoming *Floating in A Most Peculiar Way: A Memoir* (Houghton Mifflin Harcourt, 2021).**

+   **Maya Indira Ganesh is a technology researcher and writer whose work investigates the social, cultural, and political implications of the "becoming-human" of machines, and vice versa. She spent over fifteen years working at the intersec-tion of gender justice, technology, and human rights with Indian and international NGOs. She is completing a PhD at Leuphana University, Lüneburg, about the reshaping of ethics and ac-countability by the unstable ontologies of AI and autonomous systems that exist as engineering imaginaries, metaphors, and as material data infrastructures.**

+   **Wesley Goatley is a sound artist and researcher based in London. His critical practice examines the aesthetics and politics of data, machine learning, and voice recognition software technologies and the power they have in shaping the world and our understanding of it. His work is exhibited and performed internationally, including venues such as Eyebeam in New York, the Nam June Paik Art Center in Seoul, and the Victoria and Albert Museum in London. He is Course Leader of MA Interaction Design Communication at the London College of Communication, University of the Arts London.**

+   **Luciana Parisi's research is a philosophical investigation of technology in culture, aesthetics, and politics. She is a Professor in Media Philosophy at the Program in Literature and the Computational Media Art and Culture at Duke University. She is the author of *Abstract Sex: Philosophy, Biotechnology and the Mutations of Desire* (2004) and *Contagious Architecture. Computation, Aesthetics and Space* (2013). She is completing a monograph on alien epistemologies and the transformation of logical thinking in computation.**

+   **Sascha Pohflepp (1978–2019) was an artist and design researcher whose work has been known to probe the role of technology in efforts to understand and influence the environment. His interest extended across historical aspects and visions of the future, and his practice often involved collaboration with other artists and researchers. Notable exhibitions include *Talk To Me* at MoMA, New York (2011), *Micro Impact* at Museum Boijmans Van Beuningen, Rotterdam (2012), and *The House in the Sky* at Pioneer Works, New York (2016). Pohflepp lived and worked between Berlin and La Jolla, California.**

+ Sophia Roosth is an anthropologist who writes about the contemporary life sciences. In her book *Synthetic: How Life Got Made* (2017), Roosth asks what happens to "life" as a conceptual category when experimentation and fabrication converge. Grounded in an ethnographic study of synthetic biologists, she documents the profound shifts biology has undergone in the post-genomic age. She is currently a fellow at the Cullman Center for Scholars and Writers at the New York Public Library.

+ Xavier Le Roy works as choreographer and is currently Professor at the Institute for Applied Theatre Studies in Gießen. He was artist in residence at Podewil, Berlin, associated artist at the Centre chorégraphique national de Montpellier, and artist in residence fellow at the MIT Program in Art Culture and Technology in Cambridge, MA. His works produce situations that explore the relationships between spectators, visitors, performers and the emergence of subjectivities. Together with Scarlet Yu he developed the Choreography for the HKW-event *Life Forms* in 2019.

+ Gary Tomlinson is John Hay Whitney Professor of Music and Humanities at Yale University. His books, *A Million Years of Music: The Emergence of Human Modernity* (2015) and *Culture and the Course of Human Evolution* (2018), uncover deep patterns and processes in the evolutionary interaction of culture and biology; they merge biologists' "niche construction" theory with systematic analyses of Paleolithic cultures and a trans-species semiotics indebted to Charles Sanders Peirce.

Das Neue Alphabet (The New Alphabet) is a publication series by HKW (Haus der Kulturen der Welt).

The series is part of the HKW project *Das Neue Alphabet* (2019–2022), supported by the Federal Government Commissioner for Culture and the Media due to a ruling of the German Bundestag.

Series Editors: Detlef Diederichsen, Anselm Franke, Katrin Klingan, Daniel Neugebauer, Bernd Scherer
Project Management: Philipp Albers
Managing Editor: Martin Hager
Copy-Editing: Mandi Gomez, Hannah Sarid de Mowbray
Design Concept: Olaf Nicolai with Malin Gewinner and Hannes Drißner

Vol. 3: *Echo*
Editors: Nick Houde, Katrin Klingan, Johanna Schindler
Coordination: Niklas Hoffmann-Walbeck
Contributors: Lisa Baraitser, Louis Chude-Sokei, Maya Indira Ganesh, Wesley Goatley, Xavier Le Roy, Luciana Parisi, Sascha Pohflepp, Sophia Roosth, Gary Tomlinson
Photographies, *Life Forms*, Haus der Kulturen der Welt, April 25–27, 2019: Joachim Dette
Graphic Design: Malin Gewinner, Hannes Drißner, Markus Dreßen
Type-Setting: Hannah Witte
DNA-Lettering (Cover): Sören Sandbothe
Fonts: FK Raster (Florian Karsten), Suisse BP Int'l (Ian Party), Lyon Text (Kai Bernau)
Image Editing: Scancolor Reprostudio GmbH, Leipzig
Printing and Binding: Gutenberg Beuys Feindruckerei GmbH, Langenhagen

Published by:
Spector Books
Harkortstr. 10
01407 Leipzig,
www.spectorbooks.com

isn't lost

together

Distribution:
Germany, Austria: GVA Gemeinsame Verlagsauslieferung
Göttingen GmbH & Co. KG, www.gva-verlage.de
Switzerland: AVA Verlagsauslieferung AG, www.ava.ch
France, Belgium: Interart Paris, www.interart.fr
UK: Central Books Ltd, www.centralbooks.com
USA, Canada, Central and South America, Africa:
ARTBOOK | D.A.P. www.artbook.com
Japan: twelvebooks, www.twelve-books.com
South Korea: The Book Society, www.thebooksociety.org
Australia, New Zealand: Perimeter Distribution,
www.perimeterdistribution.com

Haus der Kulturen der Welt
John-Foster-Dulles-Allee 10
D-10557 Berlin
www.hkw.de

Haus der Kulturen der Welt is a business division of Kultur-
veranstaltungen des Bundes in Berlin GmbH (KBB).

Director: Bernd Scherer
Managing Director: Charlotte Sieben
Chairwoman of the Supervisory Board: Federal
Government Commissioner for Culture and the Media
Prof. Monika Grütters MdB

Haus der Kulturen der Welt is supported by

First Edition
Printed in Germany
ISBN: 978–3–95905–457–7

Already published:
Vol. 1: *The New Alphabet*
Vol. 2: *Listen to Lists!*
Vol. 3: *Counter_Readings of the Body*
Vol. 4: *Echo*

Will be published soon:
Vol. 5: *Skin and Code* (March 2021)
Vol. 6: *Carrier Bag Fiction* (April 2021)
Vol. 7: *Making* (May 2021)

Vol. 5:   *Skin and Code*
Editor: Daniel Neugebauer
Contrib.:   Alyk Blue, Johanna Burai, Luce deLire, i-PÄD,
    Rhea Ramjohn, Calah P Toussaint-Amat,
    Julia Velkova & Anne Kaun
ISBN: 978-3-95905-461-4
    March 2021

Just as physical violence leaves its marks on the skin, conceptual violence is written into interfaces via algorithms—in the form of biases turned into pixels, as discrimination implanted in memes in secret chat groups. The coding and decoding of body surfaces and interfaces is contingent on a whole host of norms. Yet these are not fixed: rather, they combine to create a matrix of tastes, cultural influences, technical conditions, and physical possibilities. The essays in this volume produce an interdisciplinary noise between surface structures and a selection of cavities: surfaces, skins, and interfaces are injured, gauged, altered, or remedied.

Vol. 6:   *Carrier Bag Fiction*
Editors: Sarah Shin, Mathias Zeiske
Contrib.:   Federico Campagna, Dorothee Elmiger,
    Ursula K. Le Guin, Enis Maci, Leanne Betasamosake
    Simpson, Anna Lowenhaupt Tsing, a. o.
ISBN: 978-3-95905-463-8
    April 2021

What if humanity's primary inventions were not the Hero's spear but rather a basket of wild oats, a medicine bundle, a story. Ursula K. Le Guin's 1986 essay *The Carrier Bag Theory of Fiction* presents a feminist story of technology that centres on the collective sustenance of life, and reimagines the carrier bag as a tool for telling strangely realistic fictions. New writings and images respond to Le Guin's narrative practice of world-making through gathering and holding.

Vol. 7:	***Making***
Editors:	Nick Houde, Katrin Klingan, Johanna Schindler
Contrib.:	Luis Campos, Maria Chehonadskih, Reece Cox, Ana Guzmán, Hao Liang, Hu Fang, Elisabeth Povinelli, Kaushik Sunder Rajan, Sophia Roosth
ISBN	978-3-95905-465-2
	May 2021

Who produces what, and how? What tools and technologies, what values and intentions are fed into the process? What part do power and control play in the context of semi-autonomous technologies that will shape our future world? The book's essays, conversations, and artist contributions focus on the practices and politics of production as a response to our contemporary processes of planetary transformation.